WOULD YOU RATHER?

HALLOWEEN EDITION

RIDDLELAND

TABLE OF CONTENTS

CHAPTER 1:
COSTUME
CATASTROPHES

WELCOME TO WANDA'S WILD COSTUME EMPORIUM, HOME OF THE WACKIEST, MOST UNPREDICTABLE HALLOWEEN OUTFITS IN TOWN! WARNING: SIDE EFFECTS MAY INCLUDE SNEEZING GLITTER, SPONTANEOUS DANCING, AND TURNING INTO A WALKING JELLYBEAN. READY TO TRY SOME ON? TOO LATE, YOU ALREADY DID. LET THE COSTUME CHAOS BEGIN!

Would you rather get stuck in a cardboard robot suit with no arm movement **OR** a ghost sheet that keeps getting blown away by the wind?

Would you rather wear a glittery unicorn costume that sneezes sparkles **OR** a hot dog costume that randomly says "Delicious!" in a deep voice?

Would you rather be a spaghetti monster with dangling noodles that wiggle **OR** a scarecrow whose costume keeps attracting real birds?

Would you rather wear a magical wizard costume that makes you float a few inches off the ground **OR** glow like a flashlight every time you laugh?

Would you rather dress as a werewolf in a sparkly tutu **OR** a ballerina with giant werewolf paws?

Would you rather dress as a banana and get followed by curious monkeys **OR** as a cat and have dogs bark at you from every yard?

Would you rather wear a pirate hat that sings sea shanties nonstop **OR** vampire fangs that chatter loudly whenever you're quiet?

Would you rather be wrapped in toilet paper like a mummy and keep unraveling **OR** be drenched in fake slime like a swamp monster?

Would you rather wear a costume made of stinky socks **OR** one made of loud, crinkly plastic bags?

Would you rather be a fairy whose wings knock things over constantly **OR** a wizard whose wand randomly shoots confetti?

Would you rather trick-or-treat as a slice of pizza
with pepperoni earrings

or a walking toilet
with a plunger hat?

Would you rather wear a
costume that smells like
candy corn all night

one that smells like gym
socks but looks super cool?

Would you rather wear a talking pumpkin on your head **OR** a wizard hat that gives terrible advice?

Would you rather dress as a frosted donut and get chased by sugar-crazed kids **OR** as a giant broccoli stalk and be totally ignored?

Would you rather wear a costume that grows leaves like a tree **OR** one that drips syrup like a pancake?

Would you rather wear a cloud costume that rains glitter **OR** a snowman suit that's freezing on the inside?

Would you rather bounce around in a jellybean costume **OR** squish through doorways in a marshmallow suit?

Would you rather be a mummy with
glow-in-the-dark wrappings

or a skeleton with bones that rattle and
dance on their own?

Would you rather
wear a knight costume
made of cooked spaghetti

OR

a dragon suit
with inflatable wings that
keep deflating?

Would you rather dress as your least favorite food and have to explain why **OR** as your weirdest dream and hope no one asks?

Would you rather be a witch whose broom keeps flying away **OR** a wizard with a beard that grows an inch every hour?

Would you rather wear a costume that turns you into a real chicken for one hour **OR** one that makes you speak only in spooky rhymes?

Would you rather wear a superhero costume made entirely of bubble wrap **OR** a witch outfit that changes colors whenever someone says "boo"?

Would you rather have a costume that gets bigger every five minutes **OR** one that slowly shrinks until you're waddling like a penguin?

Would you rather wear a taco costume that smells like melted cheese and attracts raccoons

or a zombie costume that moans "braaaains..." every time you blink?

Would you rather wear a cape that trips people  **OR** a hat that attracts every bug in the neighborhood?

Would you rather wear roller skates with every costume  squeaky shoes that alert everyone when you're sneaking candy?

Would you rather be a vampire with ketchup for blood  a werewolf who sheds furballs wherever you go?

Would you rather squeeze into a giant pumpkin suit that rolls away on hills  a vampire cape that flaps and wraps around your face every five seconds?

Would you rather wear a costume that giggles randomly  one that sneezes out confetti at awkward moments?

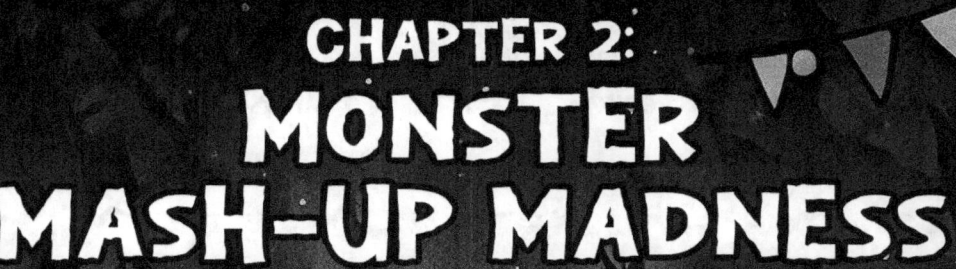

CHAPTER 2:
MONSTER
MASH-UP MADNESS

PSST! COME CLOSER; DON'T WORRY,
THE FANGED JELLYFISH ONLY BITES ON THURSDAYS. I'M
DR. WOBBLE, AND THIS IS MY MONSTER LAB, WHERE
CREATURES ARE MIXED, MASHED, ZAPPED, AND
OCCASIONALLY EXPLODE INTO RAINBOW CONFETTI. SOME
HAVE THREE EYES, OTHERS BURP GLITTER, AND ONE EVEN
TALKS THROUGH ITS BELLY BUTTON. LET'S JUST SAY...
THIS ISN'T YOUR GRANDMA'S HALLOWEEN PARTY.
READY TO MEET YOUR MONSTROUS MATCH?

Would you rather be a werewolf who howls every time someone says "candy" **OR** a vampire who can only fly in slow, dramatic circles?

Would you rather have swamp monster hair made of spaghetti noodles **OR** jellybean teeth that wiggle when you talk?

Would you rather turn invisible every time you sneeze **OR** grow a glowing eyeball on your forehead every time someone says "boo"?

Would you rather unravel like a mummy every time you laugh **OR** float through walls like a ghost whenever you get nervous?

Would you rather grow dragon wings that flap every time you tell a joke **OR** a scaly tail that knocks over everything in the kitchen?

Would you rather have monster hands that turn anything into whipped cream

or monster feet that squeak like rubber chickens?

Would you rather have a unicorn horn that glows when you're scared  bat ears that wiggle wildly when you're lying?

Would you rather grow a pumpkin head at midnight **OR** have pool noodle arms whenever you're embarrassed?

Would you rather grow vampire fangs every time you eat sugar **OR** claws that get longer the more you giggle?

Would you rather sneeze glitter so hard it knocks over decorations **OR** burp rainbows that smell like pickles?

Would you rather be a ghost who can't stop tickling people **OR** a skeleton whose bones rattle to the beat of dance music?

Would you rather grow monster feet the size of pizza boxes **OR** arms covered in neon fur that wave on their own?

Would you rather
turn into a shadow when you're scared

or into a helium balloon when you're happy?

Would you rather
have glowing monster eyes
that flash in the dark

monster ears that twitch
every time someone nearby
says "yum"?

Would you rather have bat wings that flap every time you fib **OR** a dragon tail that wags like a dog when you're hungry?

Would you rather be a two-headed monster that argues with itself **OR** a blob that splits in half when it gets tickled?

Would you rather grow fuzzy green fur all over your arms **OR** drip purple slime from your ears whenever you get excited?

Would you rather be part monster and part candy corn **OR** part monster and part giant marshmallow?

Would you rather roar like a dinosaur every time you say your name **OR** squeak like a mouse every time you walk?

Would you rather hiccup lightning bolts
like a storm beast

or sneeze out tiny bats
like an air cannon?

Would you rather have giant
monster eyebrows that
bounce when you lie

fangs that whistle every
time you try to whisper?

Would you rather leave glowing slime footprints wherever you go  make echoing monster growls every time you blink?

Would you rather turn into a mini monster when you're grumpy  into a giant one when you're excited?

Would you rather be made of Jell-O and wobble with every step  be covered in feathers and sneeze nonstop?

Would you rather be followed by a tiny monster who copies everything you say  chased by one that shouts, "Wait up!" every five seconds?

Would you rather wear a costume that makes your head spin like a top when you lie  one that makes your arms flap like chicken wings when you're nervous?

Would you rather have spider legs that let you stick to walls  a lizard tongue that grabs candy from across the room?

Would you rather be a cyclops with a blinking contest problem  a goblin with a voice that sounds like a rubber duck?

Would you rather have a costume that makes you grow taller with each joke  wider with every laugh?

Would you rather live in a haunted mansion full of talking mirrors  in a pumpkin cave guarded by a breakdancing skeleton?

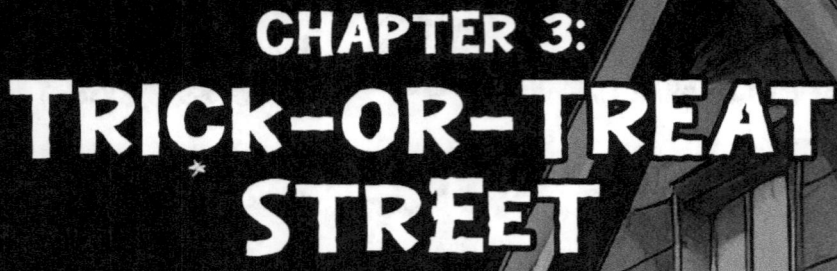

CHAPTER 3:
TRICK-OR-TREAT STREET

GOT YOUR CANDY BUCKET? GOOD. YOU'RE ABOUT TO STEP ONTO TRICK-OR-TREAT STREET, THE MOST BONKERS, MAGICAL, TREAT-FILLED NEIGHBORHOOD IN THE ENTIRE UNIVERSE. EVERY HOUSE IS DIFFERENT. SOME HAND OUT FLOATING COTTON CANDY, OTHERS SHOOT CARAMEL FROM CANNONS, AND ONE EVEN MAKES YOU DANCE FOR YOUR DESSERT. JUST REMEMBER: THE SIDEWALKS SQUISH, THE MAILBOXES TALK, AND THE CANDY MIGHT GIGGLE. READY TO KNOCK ON SOME DOORS AND TEST YOUR SWEET TOOTH BRAVERY? LET'S GO!

Would you rather knock on a door that blasts spooky fog and plays creepy pipe organ music  OR one that explodes with rainbow glitter and shouts, "WELCOME TO THE PICKLE PARTY!"?

Would you rather get a chocolate bar that whispers your secrets  OR a jawbreaker that changes flavors every time you blink?

Would you rather tiptoe down a sidewalk made of sticky caramel  OR bounce across a path of candy corn trampolines?

Would you rather get candy from a pirate who insists you say "Aye aye!" before every treat  OR from a wizard who makes you tell a riddle or lose your candy?

Would you rather carry a talking pumpkin bucket that keeps begging for more candy  OR a giant bat-shaped backpack that flaps its wings whenever you run?

Would you rather visit a house that drops candy from a mini helicopter  **OR** one where a ghost hands it to you through the door?

Would you rather be launched from house to house by a trampoline  **OR** ride a slow-moving parade float shaped like a haunted banana?

Would you rather knock on a door that opens into a room of dancing skeletons  **OR** one where you get chased by a giggling pumpkin?

Would you rather be followed by a floating eyeball that yells "LEFT TURN!" **OR** a broomstick that tries to race you to each house?

Would you rather get candy shaped like eyeballs that blink  **OR** gummy worms that slither off your hand before you eat them?

Would you rather walk down a block made of glowing marshmallows

or one made entirely of slippery banana peels?

Would you rather trick-or-treat with shoes that honk every time you take a step  with a hat that keeps yelling "CANDY DETECTED!"?

Would you rather visit a house where candy rains from the roof  one where you grab it from a treasure chest guarded by a snoring ogre?

Would you rather only be able to say "trick-or-treat" while singing opera  while doing the chicken dance?

Would you rather collect candy that glows in the dark  candy that tells corny Halloween jokes?

Would you rather ride a flying scooter between houses  bounce from doorstep to doorstep on a pogo pumpkin?

Would you rather have a candy bucket that burps every time you add more  one that randomly sings "It's Raining Gummy Bears"?

Would you rather be handed a caramel apple
by a robot with butterfingers

or a gummy bear from a vampire with hiccups?

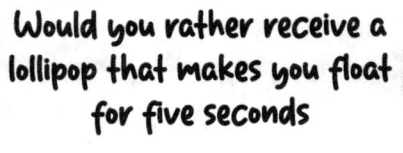

Would you rather receive a
lollipop that makes you float
for five seconds

a candy cane
that makes your
voice echo like a cave?

Would you rather be asked to tell a joke at every house  be challenged to make a spooky face before getting candy?

Would you rather get only weird candy like garlic gum and pickle pops  candy that looks normal but randomly yells "BOO!" when you chew it?

Would you rather every streetlight turn into a glowing eyeball that follows you  every mailbox laugh when you walk by?

Would you rather accidentally swap costumes with a ghost halfway down the street  with a squirrel who LOVES candy?

Would you rather go trick-or-treating with a fog machine that follows you everywhere  with a bubble blower that makes spooky shapes?

Would you rather wear gloves that
turn everything you touch into bubble gum

or shoes that stick to the ground after every step?

Would you rather knock on
a door and be sprayed with
glitter before you get candy  be tickled by invisible
feathers as you walk away?

Would you rather visit a house with a trampoline porch  one with a haunted hammock that giggles when you sit down?

Would you rather end the night with a candy pile so big it needs its own chair  one that magically refills itself every time you give a piece away?

Would you rather get one candy the size of a soccer ball  a hundred tiny candies that won't stop singing "Trick-or-Treat and Repeat"?

Would you rather every house play spooky music when you arrive  shoot streamers from the chimney when you leave?

CHAPTER 4:
HAUNTED HOUSE HAPPENINGS

DARE TO ENTER? JUST KIDDING... SORT OF. WELCOME TO
THE HAUNTED HOUSE OF HILARIOUS HORRORS!
HERE, THE COUCHES GROWL, THE TOILETS CHEER, AND THE
CHANDELIERS MIGHT SNEEZE GLITTER ON YOUR HEAD.
THE WALLS WHISPER, THE FLOORS GIGGLE,
AND ONE BROOM KEEPS FOLLOWING YOU AROUND.
TIPTOE IF YOU MUST, BUT DON'T BE SURPRISED IF
THE CLOSET STARTS DANCING.
LET'S EXPLORE, ONE CREAKY, KOOKY ROOM AT A TIME!

Would you rather open a door that fills the room with foggy giggles **OR** one that blasts spooky jazz every time you blink?

Would you rather walk down a hallway where the floor squishes like jelly **OR** where the paintings whisper weird compliments like "Nice elbows!"?

Would you rather sit on a couch that growls when you relax **OR** a chair that slides away every time you try to sit down?

Would you rather get trapped in a room that floats gently like a balloon **OR** one that bounces like a trampoline whenever you take a step?

Would you rather meet a ghost who wants to read you their diary **OR** one who won't stop telling terrible knock-knock jokes?

Would you rather open a closet and
be buried in spaghetti noodles

or have a flock of dancing rubber chickens jump out?

Would you rather
tiptoe through a hallway
where the lights flicker
every time you giggle

one where every step
makes a different
cartoon sound?

Would you rather explore an attic where furniture floats around singing opera **OR** a basement where invisible stairs play hide-and-seek?

Would you rather brush your teeth in a bathroom where the mirror tells embarrassing stories **OR** where the toilet cheers like a sports announcer?

Would you rather sneak through a room that makes fart noises with every step **OR** one where chandeliers sneeze glitter on your head?

Would you rather be chased by a vacuum cleaner with googly eyes **OR** a pile of socks that giggle and stick to your shoes?

Would you rather wear socks that scream when you dance **OR** slippers that argue about which way to turn?

Would you rather eat ghost cupcakes
that taste like clouds

or haunted popcorn that screams "Pick me!"
every time you reach for it?

Would you rather
nap in a bedroom where
everything is upside down

one where the bed floats
and spins like a lazy
carousel?

Would you rather discover a hallway full of ticklish skeletons  a room filled with bouncing eyeballs that tell jokes?

Would you rather sleep in a bed that floats two feet off the ground  one that gently rocks like a jelly boat?

Would you rather brush your teeth with ghost toothpaste that makes your smile glow  pumpkin paste that smells like cinnamon cookies?

Would you rather take a bubble bath where the bubbles giggle  a shower where the water sings opera in squirrel voices?

Would you rather play hide-and-seek with invisible ghosts  tag with a flying pair of shoes that won't stop spinning?

Would you rather be stuck in a library
with burping books

or in a kitchen where the cabinets moo
when you open them?

Would you rather
open the fridge to find
blinking candy eyeballs

OR

open the freezer and
get serenaded by
singing popsicles?

Would you rather pet a haunted cat that turns into fog when startled  a dog that barks only in ghost riddles?

Would you rather walk into a room where candy rains from the ceiling  where the floor plays spooky music like a piano when you step?

Would you rather open a drawer that growls "Nope!"  a cabinet that asks weird personal questions like, "Did you floss today?"

Would you rather have the haunted house shrink into a dollhouse while you're inside  expand into a maze of floating candy rooms?

Would you rather befriend a shy ghost who hides in your backpack  a bold one who narrates everything you do like a movie trailer?

Would you rather be greeted by a spooky butler who only speaks in riddles  a talking pumpkin who yells your name every 30 seconds?

Would you rather hear spooky lullabies from under the bed  see blinking googly eyes peeking from the ceiling tiles?

Would you rather have your voice echo in spooky whispers  randomly switch to a dramatic werewolf howl?

Would you rather exit the haunted house through a slide shaped like a dragon's tongue  bounce out on a trampoline into a pit of glow-in-the-dark marshmallows?

CHAPTER 5:
CANDY CONUNDRUMS

YOU MADE IT TO THE TASTIEST PART OF HALLOWEEN, BUT DON'T LET YOUR SWEET TOOTH GET TOO CONFIDENT. ON THIS STREET, THE LOLLIPOPS LAUGH, THE JELLYBEANS BOUNCE, AND THE CHOCOLATE BARS... MIGHT BE ALIVE. SOME TREATS COME WITH MAGICAL SIDE EFFECTS. OTHERS MIGHT STICK TO YOUR HEAD, CHANGE YOUR VOICE, OR CHASE YOU AROUND THE ROOM. ONE EVEN GROWLED AT ME ONCE. BUCKLE UP, CANDY CRUSADER:
IT'S ABOUT TO GET STICKY.

Would you rather eat a jellybean that makes you float like a balloon for ten seconds  one that makes you spin in circles like a candy top?

Would you rather unwrap a chocolate bar that sings show tunes with every bite  one that whispers your name when you're not looking?

Would you rather bite into a candy apple that crackles like fireworks  one that squeaks like a rubber duck?

Would you rather eat a gummy worm that slithers around your plate  a sour candy that makes your tongue glow in the dark?

Would you rather snack on ghost-shaped marshmallows that giggle  vampire gummies that pretend to bite your fingers?

Would you rather every candy you eat turn your teeth a different color  your eyebrows into candy canes?

Would you rather lick a lollipop that changes flavor with every step you take  one that randomly shouts "SPOOKY SNACK TIME!" at full volume?

Would you rather eat candy that makes you bounce like a gummy kangaroo  one that makes you laugh uncontrollably every time someone says "trick"?

Would you rather eat a caramel that glues your fingers together  a licorice rope that ties your shoelaces on its own?

Would you rather unwrap a piece of candy that asks riddles before it lets you eat it  one that tells bad puns every time you chew?

Would you rather chew gum that inflates a bubble big enough to lift your feet off the ground

or gum that explodes with glitter and smells like socks?

Would you rather find a haunted candy bucket that randomly swaps your treats  one that burps every time you add something sweet?

Would you rather carry a candy bucket that screams "MORE CANDY!" every 30 seconds  one that hums creepy lullabies after midnight?

Would you rather eat a jawbreaker that never stops spinning in your mouth  one that turns your tongue into a disco ball?

Would you rather get candy from a vampire chef who insists on seasoning everything with garlic powder  from a zombie baker who can't stop sneezing powdered sugar?

Would you rather find a cotton candy cloud that floats away when you chase it  one that sticks to your entire face like a fluffy helmet?

Would you rather trade all your candy for one giant mystery chocolate shaped like Frankenstein's foot  keep your candy but have it randomly vanish one piece at a time?

Would you rather eat a chocolate bat
that flaps its wings before melting

or a gummy eyeball that winks just
before you bite it?

Would you rather eat a
spooky snack that gives you
hiccups shaped like bats

 OR

burps that smell like
pumpkin pie?

Would you rather take a bite of mystery candy that tastes like pickles and pancakes  one that tastes amazing but makes your nose squeak?

Would you rather get stuck to your candy bag like glue  have to hold it with tongs because it keeps biting back?

Would you rather eat a sour ghost gummy that floats around your mouth  a cursed chocolate coin that won't stop telling jokes?

Would you rather have candy rain from the sky every time you sneeze  candy grow out of your backpack whenever you tell a lie?

Would you rather only be able to eat triangle-shaped candy forever  only candy that wiggles before you bite it?

Would you rather open a jack-o'-lantern and find it full of jelly

or a witch's hat stuffed with melted chocolate?

Would you rather every piece of candy sing "Happy Halloween" off-key  shout random facts about pumpkins?

Would you rather eat fudge that turns your fingers invisible for five minutes  a toffee that makes your ears wiggle when you talk?

Would you rather end Halloween night with a glowing pile of dancing jellybeans  a candy monster made entirely of everything you collected?

Would you rather find a haunted gumball machine that shoots treats at your head  one that makes you dance every time you get candy?

Would you rather chomp a cookie that makes your hair poof up like a haunted poodle  one that turns your voice into a ghostly whisper?

CHAPTER 6:
PUMPKIN PATCH PANDEMONIUM

THESE PUMPKINS DON'T JUST SIT AROUND; THEY BOUNCE, GLOW, BURP, AND DANCE THE CHA-CHA UNDER A FULL MOON. ONE HUMS LULLABIES. ANOTHER KEEPS TRYING TO SELL YOU INSURANCE. AND A FEW ARE DEFINITELY PLOTTING SOMETHING WEIRD BEHIND THE SCARECROW. SO GRAB YOUR FLASHLIGHT, WATCH YOUR SHOELACES, AND PREPARE FOR THE SILLIEST, SLIMIEST, MOST UNPREDICTABLE PUMPKIN ADVENTURE OF YOUR LIFE.

Would you rather ride a giant pumpkin that bounces like a trampoline  one that spins like a merry-go-round while giggling nonstop?

Would you rather carve a pumpkin that sneezes glitter whenever you touch it  one that tells spooky jokes as you scoop its guts?

Would you rather wear a pumpkin helmet that lights up when you lie  one that shouts, "Trick or treat, my dude!" every time you blink?

Would you rather eat pumpkin pie that makes you burp cinnamon-scented bubbles  drink pumpkin juice that turns your hair bright orange for an hour?

Would you rather roll down a hill inside a giant pumpkin yelling "WHEEEE!"  bounce across a patch full of slippery pumpkin guts that go splorch every time you land?

Would you rather meet a pumpkin that thinks it's a dog and chases squirrels

or one that dances whenever it hears spooky music?

Would you rather have pumpkins grow on your arms like gloves that squeak  OR on your feet like shoes that leave glowing footprints?

Would you rather be chased by a pumpkin on rollerblades, throwing candy  one riding a unicycle while juggling glow sticks?

Would you rather grow a pumpkin mustache that tickles your nose when you talk  pumpkin eyebrows that twitch every time you fib?

Would you rather visit a patch where pumpkins whisper your secrets to butterflies  one where they try to guess your favorite candy by humming?

Would you rather wear pumpkin pants that squeak like rubber ducks  a pumpkin backpack that hums "Monster Mash" when it's full?

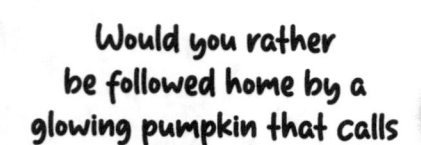

Would you rather be followed home by a glowing pumpkin that calls you "Captain Candy"  one that giggles and rolls away every time you try to pick it up?

Would you rather enter a pumpkin maze where the walls giggle when touched

or one where the floor wobbles like jelly with every step?

Would you rather get stuck inside a talking pumpkin that keeps complimenting your socks  one that dramatically reads spooky poetry in a British accent?

Would you rather juggle three tiny pumpkins that bounce like basketballs  OR carry one giant pumpkin that sings opera when it's bored?

Would you rather grow pumpkin fingers that leave trails of cinnamon dust  OR pumpkin toes that squeak like toy ducks when you walk?

Would you rather meet a wizard who turns everything you touch into pumpkins  OR a witch who only speaks in rhyming pumpkin puns?

Would you rather wear a crown made of mini glowing pumpkins  OR a cloak that smells like roasted pumpkin seeds every time you twirl?

Would you rather have to name 20 pumpkins in 30 seconds  OR do a dance battle with a pumpkin wearing sunglasses and a gold chain?

Would you rather play dodgeball with
bouncing pumpkins that laugh when hit

or soccer with a pumpkin that keeps growing legs
and running away?

Would you rather
find a pumpkin that grants
one silly wish

OR

one that fills your shoes
with jellybeans every time
you say "please"?

Would you rather jump into a pile of tiny pumpkins that squeal when squished  roll around in a bubble bath that smells like pumpkin pie and giggles when stirred?

Would you rather decorate a pumpkin that changes facial expressions every minute  one that randomly burps glitter when no one's looking?

Would you rather get chased by a squad of cheerleading pumpkins  one giant pumpkin in a cape that insists it's "Pumpkin Man"?

Would you rather carry a pumpkin that hums spooky music and glows  one that shouts "BOO!" every time you try to run?

Would you rather eat a pumpkin that tastes like cotton candy but smells like pickles  one that tastes like chocolate but squeaks when you chew?

Would you rather plant a pumpkin seed that explodes into confetti when it sprouts  one that grows candy vines every time you sneeze near it?

Would you rather pick a pumpkin that sings opera every time it's picked up  one that won't stop telling knock-knock jokes about squirrels?

Would you rather end Halloween night with a glowing pumpkin parade led by dancing vines  a sleepover inside a giant jack-o'-lantern that snores?

Would you rather discover a pumpkin that turns into a pogo stick  one that morphs into a trampoline made of licorice?

CHAPTER 7:
SPOOKY SCHOOL SHENANIGANS

WELCOME TO GHOULSTONE ELEMENTARY, WHERE THE LOCKERS WHISPER, THE HALLWAYS FLOAT, AND YOUR SUBSTITUTE TEACHER MIGHT BE A VAMPIRE WEARING GYM SHORTS. THE CAFETERIA FOOD WIGGLES, THE SPELLING TESTS VANISH, AND THE SCHOOL BELL DOESN'T RING: IT HOWLS. SO GRAB YOUR GHOST-PROOF BACKPACK, KEEP YOUR WAND IN YOUR PENCIL CASE, AND DON'T TRUST THE WATER FOUNTAIN. CLASS IS IN SESSION... MAYBE.

Would you rather open your locker and get sprayed with neon slime  hear it yell "Homework alert!" every time you pass by?

Would you rather ride a flying desk to class  get dragged around the halls by a backpack that thinks it's a racecar?

Would you rather use pencils that doodle haunted houses on their own  notebooks that hiss when you make a mistake?

Would you rather sit next to a ghost who won't stop humming  a vampire who keeps stealing your juice boxes?

Would you rather open your lunchbox and find a sandwich that tries to escape  spaghetti that floats in midair and waves at people?

Would you rather carry a backpack that randomly burps  wear shoes that leave behind glowing slime footprints?

Would you rather get stuck using glue that makes your hands sparkle forever  scissors that sing spooky songs every time they snip?

Would you rather answer a math question while riding a bouncing chair  while being tickled by ghost feathers?

Would you rather eat pudding that cackles when you poke it  stew that bubbles and changes colors every few seconds?

Would you rather have a teacher who levitates when mad  one whose shadow sneaks off to the vending machine during class?

Would you rather have a gym teacher
who turns into a werewolf during dodgeball

or a music teacher who only speaks in ghostly opera?

Would you rather be
sent to detention with
a growling pumpkin who
insists it's the principal

with a skeleton
who keeps losing his limbs?

Would you rather hear the bell howl like a werewolf  OR giggle like a baby ghost whenever it rings?

Would you rather earn extra credit by juggling eyeball-shaped jelly  by moonwalking past the principal's office?

Would you rather open your locker and find it filled with singing bats  dancing glow sticks that never turn off?

Would you rather eat lunch at a table that tells jokes  one that tries to steal your napkins?

Would you rather have a teacher with glow-in-the-dark eyes  one who floats upside down while teaching?

Would you rather walk through a hallway
where every locker blinks

or where every backpack growls
when you look at it?

Would you rather play tag
in a gym filled with
floating fog

 OR

hide-and-seek in a library
where books rearrange
themselves constantly?

Would you rather raise your hand and accidentally summon bats  get applauded by invisible students every time you answer a question?

Would you rather take a reading class where the books whisper creepy rhymes  an art class where the paint keeps sneezing?

Would you rather write with a pen that argues back  a tablet that randomly changes all your answers into Halloween jokes?

Would you rather serve detention with a ghost who wants to practice his stand-up comedy  with a werewolf who insists on yoga time?

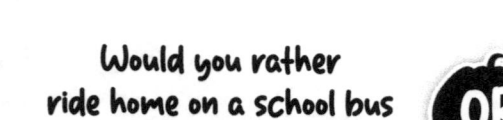

Would you rather ride home on a school bus that talks in riddles  one that hiccups glitter every time it hits a bump?

Would you rather be chased by a flying eraser that leaves chalk dust trails

or by a highlighter that squeals when it gets near you?

Would you rather wear socks that howl  shoes that randomly burst into spooky music during class?

Would you rather sit in a chair that spins uncontrollably  one that bounces like a trampoline every time you raise your hand?

Would you rather have to take a quiz where the questions float around the room  one where they're written in disappearing ink?

Would you rather sit next to a witch who turns your pencils into worms  a zombie who keeps drooling on your quiz?

Would you rather end your school day with a hallway flash mob of dancing mops  a confetti-blasting report card that sings your grades?

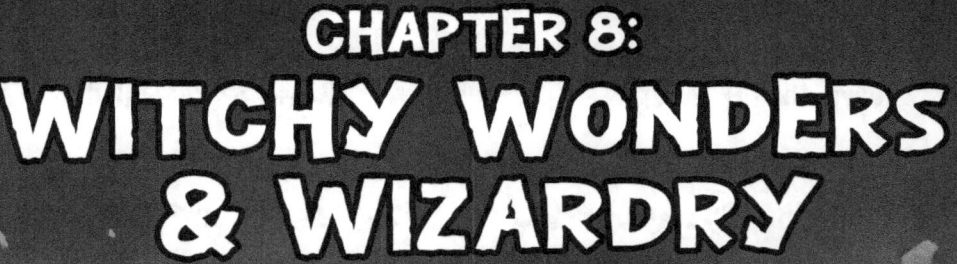

CHAPTER 8:
WITCHY WONDERS & WIZARDRY

SO YOU MADE IT TO BROOMSTICK ACADEMY? CONGRATS!
NOW DODGE THE BURPING CAULDRONS, GRAB A WAND
THAT DOESN'T EXPLODE (HOPEFULLY), AND TRY NOT TO
TRIP OVER THE SELF-STIRRING POTIONS. ONE CLASS
TEACHES BROOM RACING, ANOTHER TEACHES BAT
WHISPERING, AND SOMEONE DEFINITELY JUST TURNED
THEIR DESK INTO A LLAMA. MAGIC HERE IS MESSY,
UNPREDICTABLE, AND A WHOLE LOT OF FUN.
READY TO CAST SOME TROUBLE?

Would you rather ride a broom that sneezes glitter every time it takes off  one that zooms off without warning while shouting "YEEHAW!"?

Would you rather have a wand that shoots jellybeans instead of spells  one that accidentally turns your shoes into waffles?

Would you rather cast a spell that makes you levitate but only while doing the chicken dance  one that turns you invisible whenever you sneeze?

Would you rather have a talking cauldron that never stops giving life advice  a spellbook that growls every time you touch it?

Would you rather accidentally turn your teacher into a frog  your homework into a swarm of flying candy corn?

Would you rather wear enchanted boots
that randomly tap dance

or gloves that puff out pink smoke when you wave?

Would you rather attend
potion class with a sleepy
wizard who mumbles spells

a witch who sings
everything like
she's in a musical?

Would you rather wear a hat that sings show tunes during tests  robes that glow when you're nervous and flash when you're lying?

Would you rather accidentally summon 100 hyperactive fairies who won't stop decorating you  one grumpy pumpkin who moves into your room and demands snacks?

Would you rather have a wand that changes colors depending on your mood  one that randomly turns objects into pancakes on Wednesdays?

Would you rather be stuck in a class where every word is spoken backward  one where everyone speaks only in meows?

Would you rather cast a spell that makes everyone float like balloons  one that turns backpacks into barking puppies?

Would you rather fly on a broomstick
that hiccups midair

or on a magic carpet that keeps trying to nap?

Would you rather get
caught in a glitter explosion
that follows you for a week

OR

drink a potion that
makes your burps sound like
ghostly whispers?

Would you rather
wear socks that make you
hover above the ground  shoes that sing
the alphabet
while you walk?

Would you rather
be turned into a toad
for 10 minutes  have sparkly
unicorn horns randomly
appear on your elbows?

Would you rather cast a
spell that makes everyone
break into dance  one that makes cupcakes
shout "Pick me!"
from the table?

Would you rather
try to catch a runaway
crystal ball that
rolls around giggling  chase a wand that hides
behind furniture?

Would you rather
share a desk with a dragon
who snores fire  a unicorn who
won't stop asking riddles
during class?

Would you rather drink a potion that makes your voice sound like a trumpet

or one that gives you a tail that wags when you lie?

Would you rather enter a magical duel where you can only cast bubble spells  one where you must wear oven mitts the entire time?

Would you rather have a magic hat that randomly shouts embarrassing facts  a wand that keeps zapping your shoelaces undone?

Would you rather ride a broom that plays bagpipe music nonstop  one that only turns left; and loudly announces it each time?

Would you rather have a pet toad that copies everything you say in a British accent  a cat that rolls its eyes every time you mess up a spell?

Would you rather mix a potion that makes everyone hiccup bubbles  one that makes them moo like cows when they sit down?

Would you rather compete in a spell-casting contest where spells keep sneezing glitter  a potion-mixing race judged by cranky gnomes?

Would you rather have a wand that flings spaghetti when startled  one that laughs every time you say "abracadabra"?

Would you rather have your wand replaced with a bendy spaghetti noodle  your cauldron replaced with a singing teapot named Mervin?

Would you rather end the school day with a surprise wand duel in the cafeteria  a flying broom parade led by a breakdancing wizard?

Would you rather accidentally turn your voice into honking goose sounds  your hands into clouds that make fart noises?

CHAPTER 9:
CREEPY-CRAWLY CRITTERS

YES, IT'S SLIMY. AND YES, SOMETHING JUST BUZZED PAST YOUR EAR WEARING A TUTU AND YELLING, "WATCH MY CARTWHEEL!" WELCOME TO THE LAND OF SCUTTLES, SQUEAKS, AND SUSPICIOUS SLIME. HERE, SPIDERS KNIT SWEATERS, CENTIPEDES WEAR ROLLER SKATES, AND WORMS FORM BOY BANDS. SOME BUGS ARE SWEET. SOME ARE SNEAKY. ONE MIGHT BE LIVING IN YOUR PENCIL CASE AND WRITING ITS MEMOIR. READY TO DIVE INTO THE MOST RIDICULOUS BUG WORLD EVER? HOPE YOU BROUGHT YOUR ITCH-PROOF SOCKS.

Would you rather wake up with glitter beetles in your hair doing jazz hands  a worm on your nose whispering compliments?

Would you rather wear shoes filled with sleepy snails that hum lullabies  gloves full of tiny frogs that keep high-fiving strangers?

Would you rather sneeze and shoot out mini crickets wearing helmets  hiccup and release butterflies that form your face in midair?

Would you rather be chased by a slime blob that wants to cuddle,  a dancing centipede who insists you join his flash mob?

Would you rather open your backpack and find it full of ants reading books  grasshoppers arguing about lunch?

Would you rather sit on a chair made of buzzing flies that argue constantly  on one made of worms that keep rearranging themselves?

Would you rather play tag with a pack of lightning-fast roly-polies  hide-and-seek with ninja crickets?

Would you rather be followed everywhere by a cheering line of ants with pom-poms  a bat who writes theme songs about your life?

Would you rather eat cookies that crawl off your plate and hide behind the couch  candy that giggles, unwraps itself, and runs away yelling "No thanks!"?

Would you rather babysit a glowworm who only speaks in riddles  a stinkbug who thinks he's royalty and demands a throne?

Would you rather brush your teeth with
caterpillar toothpaste that giggles

or wash your face with slug slime
that smells like cupcakes?

Would you rather
win a pie-eating contest
judged by mosquitoes

 OR

a dance battle hosted
by glow-in-the-dark
roaches?

Would you rather raise a caterpillar who becomes a famous opera singer  a fly who's really into modern dance?

Would you rather attend a fancy insect tea party where everyone wears tiny hats  a bug rock concert where the mosh pit is made of bouncing beetles?

Would you rather take a bubble bath with polite leeches who compliment your singing  bathe in lime-scented slime with floating gummy spiders?

Would you rather open your cereal box and find a spider wearing a monocle  a centipede doing yoga on your spoon?

Would you rather have a cricket in your pencil case that critiques your handwriting  a worm that rewrites your notes in emoji?

Would you rather be locked in a room
with a debating team of beetles

or go to a sleepover with giggling scorpions
who love karaoke?

Would you rather
slip on slug tracks
that squeak

fall into a puddle of
giggling jellyfish who tickle
you on purpose?

Would you rather wear a cape made of moth wings that flutters wildly  **OR** a crown of glowworms that keeps changing colors based on your mood?

Would you rather get slimed by a jelly slug that sings lullabies  **OR** a blob of mold that only speaks in pirate slang?

Would you rather have eyebrows made of worm braids  **OR** eyelashes that blink out Morse code using fireflies?

Would you rather eat jellybeans that taste like bug farts but give you super speed  **OR** cookies that taste amazing but sing off-key when chewed?

Would you rather raise a polite tarantula who becomes your life coach  **OR** a ticklish slime puddle that won't stop following you?

Would you rather chase a cockroach
riding a scooter through your kitchen

or try to catch a bat that keeps shouting
your secrets?

Would you rather
walk through a hallway
made of sticky spider webs
that play music

one filled with tiny
bouncing toads yelling
"Encore!"?

Would you rather have a spider that critiques your outfit in a French accent  a beetle that tries to brush your hair with a spoon?

Would you rather be crowned "Bug king" and have to attend daily parades  be the royal slime taster for a group of hungry toads?

Would you rather end your night with a glow-in-the-dark bug parade led by a breakdancing mantis  a slime slide party hosted by a DJ worm named Carl?

Would you rather keep a bug in your pocket that whispers sports scores  one that farts glitter every time you tell a joke?

CHAPTER 10:
GHOSTLY GIGGLES

SOME GHOSTS MOAN... BUT OTHERS TELL KNOCK-KNOCK JOKES. SOME HAUNT SPOOKY CASTLES... BUT OTHERS JUST WANT TO REDECORATE YOUR ROOM WITH GLOW-IN-THE-DARK TOILET PAPER. AROUND HERE, THE SPIRITS FLOAT, PRANK, SING OFF-KEY, AND STEAL YOUR SNACKS; SOMETIMES ALL AT ONCE. AND IF SOMETHING WHISPERS "BOO" BEHIND YOU... DON'T PANIC. IT'S PROBABLY JUST WORKING ON ITS STAND-UP ROUTINE. READY TO LAUGH YOUR SHEET OFF? LET'S GO!

Would you rather get followed by a ghost who only tells knock-knock jokes  one who plays slide whistle sound effects every time you talk?

Would you rather sleep in a haunted bed that floats and spins slowly  one that makes spooky "oooooo" sounds every time you roll over?

Would you rather be haunted by a ghost that rearranges your furniture into obstacle courses  one that fills your shoes with glitter jelly?

Would you rather have a ghost in your backpack who hides your pencils for fun  one that writes mysterious messages in your notebooks like "Bring snacks"?

Would you rather wear a hoodie that ghosts keep zipping and unzipping  a hat that floats off your head every time someone says "boo"?

Would you rather have a roommate ghost
who celebrates Halloween every day

or one who turns your alarm clock into a
screaming pumpkin?

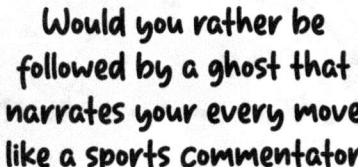

Would you rather be
followed by a ghost that
narrates your every move
like a sports commentator

one that adds dramatic
music whenever you speak?

Would you rather be spooked by a ghost who hides in your cereal box and yells, "SURPRISE!"  one who pops up in your bathroom mirror wearing sunglasses?

Would you rather go to school with a ghost who won't stop singing musical numbers  one who gives your teachers ghost-hiccups?

Would you rather hear ghostly giggles every time you open a door  get startled by invisible high-fives?

Would you rather try to play tag with a ghost who yells "BOO!" and vanishes  one who plays hide-and-seek and never gives up, even during dinner?

Would you rather have a ghost cat that purrs while floating through walls  a ghost dog that burps fog and chases invisible mail carriers?

Would you rather wear pajamas that ghosts
can pass through to tickle you

or slippers that squeak "BOO"
every time you walk?

Would you rather read a
haunted comic book that
adds you into the story

use a ghost pencil
that draws embarrassing
doodles by itself?

Would you rather ride a ghost school bus that drives through clouds  one that tells spooky riddles over the loudspeaker?

Would you rather take a bath where ghost bubbles spell silly words  brush your teeth with toothpaste that screams "MINTY!" after every squirt?

Would you rather be haunted by a ghost who finishes your sentences... incorrectly  one who randomly shouts your name like a game show host?

Would you rather have your photo photobombed by a ghost making duck faces  one that gives you glowing red eyes in every picture?

Would you rather host a ghost sleepover where everyone floats in sleeping bags  a ghost dance party with invisible disco balls?

Would you rather walk through a haunted house
where all the furniture dances

or one where the pictures wink and
stick out their tongues?

Would you rather
be haunted by a
polite ghost who applauds
everything you do

a sassy ghost
who critiques
your fashion choices?

Would you rather try to eat ghost cupcakes that float out of reach  ghost pizza that keeps turning invisible mid-bite?

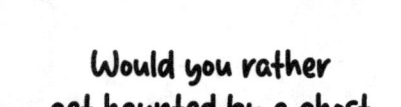

Would you rather get haunted by a ghost who sings everything they say like an opera  one who only communicates through interpretive dance?

Would you rather open your locker to find it filled with ghost glitter OR haunted lunch leftovers that rearrange themselves into smiley faces?

Would you rather have ghost friends who prank your teacher by floating pencils OR ones who haunt the PA system with chicken impressions?

Would you rather play dodgeball with invisible ghosts who throw giggling slime balls  soccer with one who keeps floating into the goal, yelling "GOOOOAL!"

Would you rather wear ghost socks that glow and dance at night  a ghost cape that keeps trying to fly away without you?

Would you rather find a haunted diary that writes silly secrets about you  a ghost phone that only sends emojis?

Would you rather get invited to a ghost tea party where the cookies vanish when you reach for them  a haunted talent show where one ghost juggles invisible frogs?

Would you rather end your night with a ghost parade of dancing sheets  a haunted comedy show hosted by a vampire in bunny slippers who only tells banana jokes?

CHAPTER 11:
MIDNIGHT MOVIE MONSTERS

IT'S MOVIE NIGHT, BUT DON'T EXPECT A QUIET SHOW. THE WEREWOLF BROUGHT NACHOS (AND ATE THE TRAY), THE MUMMY CAN'T STOP TEXTING SPOILERS, AND THE VAMPIRE IS WARMING UP FOR A DRAMATIC MONOLOGUE. AROUND HERE, MONSTERS DON'T STAY ON THE SCREEN; THEY JOIN YOU IN THE POPCORN LINE. SO GRAB YOUR TICKET (AND MAYBE A GARLIC NECKLACE), BECAUSE THIS MONSTER MASH IS MORE COMEDY THAN CATASTROPHE!

Would you rather share popcorn with a werewolf who howls at every jump scare  OR a mummy who keeps using napkins as toilet paper?

Would you rather sit next to a vampire who sings opera during quiet scenes  OR a ghost who floats in front of the screen and critiques the lighting?

Would you rather be stuck in a theater with zombies doing synchronized clapping  OR skeletons playing air guitar with their own ribs?

Would you rather star in a monster movie where you're the scream king or queen  OR play a goofy ghoul who keeps tripping over their own claws?

Would you rather have a dragon who sneezes fire at the previews  OR a swamp monster who spills grape soda on everyone in your row?

Would you rather attend a monster prom where everyone wears tuxedos with fangs  a haunted theater where the ushers are floating eyeballs?

Would you rather babysit a dragon who accidentally roasts marshmallows on everything  a yeti who's scared of popcorn kernels?

Would you rather be best friends with a nervous cyclops who wears three pairs of glasses  a shy mummy who only texts in spooky GIFs?

Would you rather direct a movie with a fashion-obsessed vampire who demands five outfit changes per scene  a robot zombie who only films in slo-mo?

Would you rather eat monster-sized gummy worms with Bigfoot  caramel corn that growls if you eat too slowly?

Would you rather arm wrestle
a polite yeti with oven mitts

or burp battle a slime creature
who smells like moldy cheese?

Would you rather
have a pet bat
that narrates your day in
dramatic movie voice

a gremlin who keeps making
slow-motion montages of
your life?

Would you rather trade lunches with a vampire who only eats beet chips  a mummy who brings a dust sandwich and labels it "vintage"?

Would you rather watch a movie where monsters throw popcorn at the screen  one where they shout your name during the scary parts?

Would you rather wear a t-shirt that says "Team Dracula" all week  have fake fangs that pop out whenever you giggle?

Would you rather be in a band with howling werewolves who only play spoons  headbang with skeletons who use their skulls as drums?

Would you rather your shadow growl every time you move  your reflection do the chicken dance whenever you wink?

Would you rather help a vampire study
for their driver's test (but no mirrors!)

or teach a zombie how to use chopsticks?

Would you rather sing
karaoke with a banshee who
only knows sea shanties

OR

dance with a ghost who
floats like a balloon and
farts glitter?

Would you rather wear Frankenstein's boots and clomp through school  have Dracula's cape that tries to fly away every time someone sneezes?

Would you rather meet a werewolf who writes sappy poetry about spaghetti  a zombie who communicates using sock puppets named "Munch" and "Chomp"?

Would you rather clean slime off your movie seat left by a swamp monster  sit through a double feature with a vampire who loudly narrates every plot twist?

Would you rather wear a monster costume that sneezes glitter every time you hiccup  one that growls "Feed me!" every hour?

Would you rather have a staring contest with a glowing cyclops who never blinks  a burping competition with a swamp ghost who smells like pickled onions?

Would you rather be pen pals with Frankenstein's monster,
who writes in crayon

or video chat with a werewolf
who only talks in howls?

Would you rather enter a
monster talent show judged
by a sarcastic vampire  one hosted by
a ghost who forgets
their lines?

Would you rather be trapped in an elevator with a werewolf who's allergic to small talk  a slime blob who keeps telling knock-knock jokes?

Would you rather get chased by a zombie on a hoverboard  a vampire who stops to check their reflection in every mirror?

Would you rather end your night with a standing ovation from tuxedo-wearing zombies  a red carpet interview hosted by glowstick-juggling skeletons?

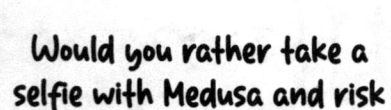

Would you rather take a selfie with Medusa and risk turning into a statue  do a TikTok dance with Dracula wearing bunny slippers?

CHAPTER 12:
HAUNTED HOLIDAY MASH-UP

WHAT HAPPENS WHEN HALLOWEEN CRASHES INTO EVERY
OTHER HOLIDAY LIKE A GLITTERY BAT OUT OF NOWHERE? PURE,
PUMPKIN-SCENTED MAYHEM! CHRISTMAS TREES WEAR VAMPIRE
CAPES, THANKSGIVING TURKEYS HAND OUT CANDY CORN, AND
THE EASTER BUNNY HIDES ZOMBIE EGGS IN HAUNTED BASKETS.
IT'S A WILD, COSTUME-MIXED, HOLIDAY-SMASHING,
CANDY-LAUNCHING CELEBRATION OF RIDICULOUS FUN. SO GRAB
YOUR CALENDAR, TOSS IT INTO A CAULDRON, AND GET READY
FOR THE SILLIEST SUGAR-STUFFED SHOWDOWN OF THE YEAR!

Would you rather trick-or-treat from an elf's sleigh pulled by flying black cats  open presents inside a haunted gingerbread mansion that giggles when you knock?

Would you rather spend Valentine's Day in a haunted heart-shaped castle  Thanksgiving dinner with ghosts who bicker about cranberry sauce?

Would you rather be chased by a Cupid who shoots chocolate slime arrows  a Thanksgiving turkey with fangs and glow-in-the-dark feathers?

Would you rather find a chocolate bunny filled with zombie jellybeans  a jack-o'-lantern stuffed with fireworks that shout "BOO!" as they burst?

Would you rather go egg hunting in a haunted graveyard where the eggs glow  trick-or-treat from the Easter Bunny, who's dressed as a pirate and hands out haunted carrots?

Would you rather carve a pumpkin
that sings carols in ghost voices

or decorate a Christmas tree
that tosses ornaments like snowballs?

Would you rather
bring a jack-o'-lantern to
the Fourth of July that
explodes into candy bats

a talking scarecrow
that sings the national
anthem backwards?

Would you rather spend New Year's Eve at a monster dance party with a disco ball made of eyeballs  at a haunted countdown where everyone floats upside-down at midnight?

Would you rather sled down a hill of candy corn with a werewolf who screams "WHEEEE!"  ice skate with a skeleton who keeps losing their legs?

Would you rather open a stocking filled with giggling bats  an Easter basket full of gummy worms that spell out riddles?

Would you rather carve a pumpkin shaped like a turkey that gobbles  wear bunny ears that scream "TRICK OR TREAT!" every time you hop?

Would you rather get pranked on April Fool's Day by a ghost who switches your socks with spaghetti  a mummy who wraps your lunch in toilet paper?

Would you rather build a snowman
that sings spooky lullabies

or one that throws snowballs
when you turn your back?

Would you rather
eat stuffing that growls like  mashed potatoes
a gremlin that levitate and swirl into
ghost shapes?

Would you rather trick-or-treat in a neighborhood made of gingerbread  one where sidewalks are chocolate but yell "YIKES!" when you step on them?

Would you rather be in a snowball fight with ice-breathing werewolves  a pie fight with goblins who yell compliments while flinging whipped cream?

Would you rather light a haunted menorah that hums creepy tunes  spin a dreidel that cackles and chases you around the room?

Would you rather play tag with invisible elves who leave glitter trails  with zombies who walk in straight lines, yelling "TAG YOU'RE IT!"?

Would you rather sled on a haunted candy cane with spooky speed  snowboard on a fruitcake that growls every time you turn?

Would you rather light fireworks with a zombie
who sneezes glitter

with a vampire who insists on narrating
every spark like a movie trailer?

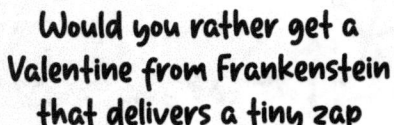

Would you rather get a
Valentine from Frankenstein
that delivers a tiny zap

one from a swamp creature
that squirts perfume
made of pond water?

Would you rather go trick-or-treating in a Santa suit that yells "HO-HO-BOO!"  dress as a turkey that lays jellybeans whenever you laugh?

Would you rather get a glowing Valentine from a vampire in roller skates  a ghost-written love poem that reads itself aloud in burps?

Would you rather wear a snow globe helmet that shows spooky scenes  monster slippers that moo, howl, and giggle every step you take?

Would you rather find a dreidel that floats and paints ghost faces on the walls  a nutcracker that bites candy and sings opera?

Would you rather end Halloween with a monster fireworks show hosted by zombie cheerleaders  a snowstorm where every flake is shaped like a bat and tastes like marshmallow?

Would you rather decorate Halloween cookies with Santa using slime-frosting  wrap gifts with Dracula, who uses cobwebs instead of ribbon?

Would you rather get candy hearts that scream "BOO, Valentine!" when you bite them  floating ghost valentines that blow garlic-scented kisses?

Would you rather sing Halloween carols to skeletons on Christmas  pass out chocolate spiders to carolers dressed as zombies?

Would you rather invent your own holiday, FrankenCandy Day, where everyone wears pajamas and eats dessert for breakfast  BOO-gust, a whole month of costumes, candy, glow-in-the-dark slime fights, and floating parade floats?

Did you enjoy the book?

If you did, we are ecstatic. If not, please write your complaint to us and we will ensure we fix it.

If you're feeling generous, there is something important that you can help me with – tell other people that you enjoyed the book.

Ask a grown-up to write about it on Amazon. When they do, more people will find out about the book. It also lets Amazon know that we are making kids around the world laugh. Even a few words and ratings would go a long way.

If you have any ideas or jokes that you think are super funny, please let us know. We would love to hear from you. Our email address is -

riddleland@riddlelandforkids.com

About Riddleland

Riddleland is a mum + dad run publishing company. We are passionate about creating fun and innovative books to help children develop their reading skills and fall in love with reading. If you have suggestions for us or want to work with us, shoot us an email at
riddleland@riddlelandforkids.com

Our family's favorite quote:
"Creativity is an area in which younger people have a tremendous advantage since they have an endearing habit of always questioning past wisdom and authority."
~ Bill Hewlett

www.ingramcontent.com/pod-product-compliance
Lightning Source LLC
Chambersburg PA
CBHW071020120626
46546CB00003B/1169